A Family Life Nature Series

The Gospel According to a SNOWFLAKE

By Terry & Jean McComb

Illustrations by Vera McMurdo

TEACH Services, Inc.
PUBLISHING
www.TEACHServices.com • (800) 367-1844

World rights reserved. Portions of this book may be photocopied for evangelistic purposes.

The author assumes full responsibility for the accuracy of all facts and quotations as cited in this book. The opinions expressed in this book are the author's personal views and interpretations, and do not necessarily reflect those of the publisher.

This book is provided with the understanding that the publisher is not engaged in giving spiritual, legal, medical, or other professional advice. If authoritative advice is needed, the reader should seek the counsel of a competent professional.

All rights reserved. No part of this publication may be reproduced, stored in a retrieval system, or transmitted in any form or by any means, except for brief quotations in printed reviews, without the prior permission of the publisher. Portions of this book may be photocopied for evangelistic purposes.

Copyright© 2023 Terry & Jean McComb
Copyright© 2023 TEACH Services, Inc.
ISBN-13: 978-1-4796-1238-3 (Paperback)
ISBN-13: 978-1-4796-1239-0 ((ePub)
Library of Congress Control Number: 2023936057

Any personal website addresses that the author included are managed by the author. TEACH Services is not responsible for the accuracy or permanency of any links.

Scripture taken from the New King James Version®. Copyright © 1982 by Thomas Nelson. Used by permission. All rights reserved. Italics omitted.

Snow crystal images used by permission from Kenneth Libbrecht.

Published by

Table of Contents

Page	Nature Object	Text	Character Lesson
v	*Preface*		
6	Snow Praise	Psalms 148:7	Praise
8	Water Cycle	Psalms 147:16, 17	Freely Give & Receive
10	Cold Beauty	Psalms 147:17, 18	Be Prepared
12	Crystal Growth	Ecclesiastes 9:10	Wise use of Time
14	Falling Snow	Ecclesiastes 12:1	Urgency of Youth
16	Pollution	Psalms 119:11	Cleansing
18	Mysterious Hexagon	Job 38:22	Wisdom of God
20	Frozen Individuality	Psalms 139:14	Individuality
22	Six-Sided Crystal	James 2:12	Law of Liberty
24	A Little Thing	Luke 16:10	Little Things
26	Stored Snow	Jeremiah 18:14	Spiritual vs Human
28	Whiter than Snow	Isaiah 1:18	Forgiveness
30	Snow Changes Things	2 Corinthians 5:17	How Sinner Changes
32	Snow Armaments	Job 38:22, 23	God's Weapons
34	Warm Snow	Isaiah 26:3	Christ's Character
36	Tracks in the Snow	Proverbs 3:6	Safe Paths
38	Frozen Reservoirs	Matthew 24:37	Record of the Past
40	Crystallized Vapor	Matthew 5:14	Holy Spirit
42	Divine Design	Colossians 1:17	On-going Commands
44	God Sends Snow	Job 37:5-13	Benefits of Trials
46	United Power	John 17:21	Unity
48	Temporary Snow	Job 6:17	Temporal Values
50	Pure as Snow	Psalms 1:6, 7, 10	Pure Motives
52	White Snow	Revelation 1:14	Glory of God
54	*Appendix 1: How to Make Paper Snowflakes*		
55	*Appendix 2: How to Restore a Snowflake*		
56	*Bibliography*		
57	*The Gospel According to Creation Seminars*		

Please Notice Carefully

The book in your hands is a multi-lesson teaching device that will involve the parent, grandparent, or teacher in a family-type activity in God's Outdoor Classroom.

Each page is a stand-alone lesson that is: 1) a reading lesson, 2) a character lesson, 3) a Bible lesson, 4) a science lesson, and 5) an art lesson (color the picture) per page.

Each lesson is created to have the parent/teacher take the child outside and share the lesson by the real object of nature under study. The lesson can be tailored either up or down, based on the child's level of experience and understanding. Later have them carefully color the art opposite the text. The Practical Project accomplished outside will awaken curiosity to desire to know the Creator Who made such a wonderful object of nature.

The art page may be photocopied for classroom use but not for resale.

This resource is excellent for Sunday/Sabbath school use or Boy/Girl Scout Club devotions. VBS leaders will find these lessons very useful. Also, pastors can use these in the children's story time in the worship service. Have the child color the picture while the pastor preaches, thus doubling the attention span of any child.

"God has shown His invisible attributes, His eternal power, and divine nature, clearly by what He has made. People are without an excuse for not glorifying God as Creator and giving Him gratitude and thanks" (Romans 1:20–21, McComb paraphrase).
ENJOY!!

Dedication

This nature series is dedicated to Tom and Martha Grove. Their faith, vision and funding made possible the first printing of this nature series in 1987.

Preface

The recurring seasons, as they march across the calendar, bring their own special delight. Winter, with its brisk cold, calls hardy nature lovers to sample its frozen wonders.

One of these frozen wonders is the "simple" snowflake. In this book we shall show that the snowflake is not really simple. In God's wonder-world of nature snow has many hidden treasures which may be found by the determined.

Snow is mentioned twenty-five times in the Bible. On the following pages you may discover some of the spiritual lessons from snow. Your child may wish to color the picture after each lesson. We recommend the study of snowflakes with the aid of a magnifying glass or microscope. Sometimes microscopes may be purchased as surplus from universities, colleges, or high schools.

May the gems of truth found during this frozen season enrich your character to be as beautiful as the divine design of a snow crystal. Its frosty charms silently proclaim, "God is Love."

Snow Praise

Twirling lazily while falling some 20,000 feet out of the lead-colored sky, the miniature snow crystal landed silently on my slide covered with black velvet. Easing the slide under my fifteen-power microscope, I began to turn the focus knob while my son held a flashlight to illuminate it.

The garage door was open at our home near Beiseker, Alberta, to better absorb the subfreezing weather. Adjusting to the darkness of the microscope, I saw a silver-coated crystal of six sides focus before my eyes. Straightening to let my two sons look, I pondered, "Is this how we can answer the question God posed to the ancient Job, 'Have you entered the treasury of snow?'" The gem I had just viewed looked like it came from the treasure chest of some hidden vault. Scientifically speaking, a snowflake may be composed of as many as a thousand or more snow crystals.

What fun it is to gather snowflakes into a snowball, a snowman, or snow fort. Sleds, skis, and snowmobiles bring endless delight while giving outdoor exercise. Yet the same snow crystals, if piled deep enough, can stop a train or even cover a village.

Polar bear mothers have been seen waiting patiently at the bottom of a big cliff while watching their cubs run up to the top of the hill and slide down again. Ruth Kirk in her book, *Snow*, tells of watching a black bear slide down a hill and then lumber back up, and repeat the pleasure. Pleasure is one of the purposes of snow, but it does much more. Snow is part of the vital link of the great water system that keeps our earth green and growing.

"Let them praise the name of the Lord, for He commanded and they were created. He has also established them forever and ever; He has made a decree which shall not pass away" (Psalm 148:5, 6). Here we are told that God has other laws besides the Ten Commandments. I would like to suggest that the snow crystal—thin and six-sided—is created by God in harmony with His laws of nature.

In Psalm 148:7, 8, David continues: "Praise the Lord from the earth ... Fire and hail, snow and clouds; Stormy wind, fulfilling His word."

Did you know that snow praises the Lord? God created the snow; everything He makes is made with care. You were created with care, too. So you, along with the snow, can praise the Lord. You can praise the Lord for the lessons He has hidden in the snow.

PRACTICAL PROJECT

Place two ice cubes on a small plate at room temperature. Note the time on the clock. Find out how much time it takes for ice to turn into water at room temperature. Because of the delay of melt time, rivers flow all year long. How does this praise the Lord?

Water Cycle

Where did our spinning little crystalline saucer come from as it twirled lazily out of the gray sky? Where did it begin its journey and why? God's Word gives us this simple answer: "He gives snow like wool; He scatters the frost like ashes; he casts out His hail like morsels" (Psalm 147:16, 17).

Our frosty flying saucer did not begin it journey as a crystal, but rather as mist rising out of the ocean. This vapor is absorbed into warm air above dancing waves through a process called evaporation. Wind blows this moisture-laden air over land. Rising air cools, and as it cools, the vapor condenses into clouds.

Clouds pass over mountain ranges. Nature uses a cold hand to squeeze this cloudy sponge, when she dumps this moisture in the form of sleet, hail, rain, or snow.

Our atmosphere normally holds about ten-days' supply of fresh water suspended in air. If the clouds are high enough, the snow will compact into glaciers sleeping upon frozen peaks.

Glaciers, like giant ice cubes, slowly melt and become little rills which merge together, creating streams. Streams merge together to become rivers. Rivers channel melted snow-water back to the salty sea. Thus, this bit of moisture will have made one giant round trip ending up back home again.

Solomon knew this. "All rivers run into the sea, yet the sea is not full; to the place from which the rivers come, there they return again" (Ecclesiastes 1:7). Snow is a frosty link in the great cycle of water. Its mission was created by God. Like water, we are each part of life's great cycle of love. God gives His pure love through Jesus. We share Jesus' gift of love with our parched neighbors. They in turn give thanks back to God and praise Him for His goodness. The love cycle is then complete.

 ## PRACTICAL PROJECT

Set up a rain gauge. (You can buy one from the hardware store.) As a family, record how much rain falls during each storm. Ask: Did this water come from the Pacific Ocean or Atlantic Ocean? The North pole or South pole? On the internet, get a satellite picture of the weather. From which direction are the clouds coming? This will help you follow the rain's journey before it fell where you live.

Water Cycle

Cold Beauty

Snow is as cold as ice cream. To remain frozen it must stay at temperatures less than 32°F (0°C). When snow passes through a warmer layer of air it will turn to rain. If the air layer at ground level is thin and below freezing, then the rain will freeze when it touches a freezing object on the ground. This is called freezing rain and produces an ice storm. "He casts out His hail like morsels; who can stand before His cold? He sends out His word and melts them; He causes His wind to blow, and the waters flow" (Psalm 147:17, 18).

Who can stand before His cold? Only the one who is prepared. A mother prepares winter clothing while it is warm. When the cold arrives she is ready. "She is not afraid of snow for her household, for all her household is clothed with scarlet" (Proverbs 31:21).

Snow lasts only as long as it is cold; likewise life lasts a very short time in this world because of sin. "As drought and heat consume the snow waters, so should the grave those who have sinned" (Job 24:19).

Seasons come and go. In the hot season of summer our mountain community will send someone higher up the mountain for snow. With the cold snow we make ice cream. It is so refreshing. Solomon discovered this same refreshing truth when he wrote, "Like the cold of snow in time of harvest, is a faithful messenger to those who send him, for he refreshes the soul of his masters" (Proverbs 25:13).

If God puts this much beauty into snow which may last only for moments, what can He do with your life and mine?

 PRACTICAL PROJECT

Make a real snow cone.

Scoop freshly fallen snow into a glass. Pour a few spoonfuls of frozen grape juice concentrate on top for a purple snow cone. If it is not the snow season you can make snow by slivering ice in a blender. Place two cups of small ice cubes in a pre-chilled blender and pulse. Blend till ice is fine as possible. Working fast put shaved ice into a glass and drizzle with 2–4 tablespoons of your favorite fruit juice concentrate. Enjoy!

Crystal Growth

Growing Only Once

A typical snowflake measures less than one-half inch across and is made up of many snow crystals. A snow crystal grows by absorbing vapor from around it. One snow crystal may contain one quintillion molecules of water. These molecules crystallize together creating a beautiful snowflake.

In 1887 in Montana they measured snowflakes as big as dinner plates—15 inches across and 8 inches thick. Giant snowflakes are rare. However, record sizes of three, four, and five inches have been found in different countries during this past century. A beautiful snow crystal lasts only as long as it floats earthward. Once landed, it soon loses its crystal form which will never be seen again.

Some snowfalls are very small because there is little to no moisture in the atmosphere. Heavy snowfalls happen when air temperature is 15° Fahrenheit or -9° Celsius or warmer because this air holds more water vapor. When temperatures drop to below 0° Fahrenheit or -17° Celsius, snowflakes are smaller because at that temperature all moisture has already crystallized so there is no water vapor in the air.

Snow is like time. Moments tick away and melt into history, forever gone, never to be relived. Time measurements are similar: in sixes. Sixty seconds following each other make one minute. Sixty minutes added together form one hour. Twenty-four hours join to make a day. Seven days create one week. Four weeks make a month. Twelve months in a row form one year. So our days melt away like snow, never to return.

Solomon says we should guard the ticks of a clock, or life will be in vain. "Whatever your hand finds to do, do it with your might" (Ecclesiastes 9:10). Treasure each moment for we cannot add one second to a day, but we can keep from wasting them.

Our time counts when spent doing useful chores for mother and father. Meal preparation, cleaning, jobs around the house, all bless our parents' lives and enrich our own. By the right use of time we acquire the ability to be of useful service. As we serve, we gain self-confidence and will be welcome workers anywhere. "… Not lagging in diligence, fervent in spirit, serving the Lord" (Romans 12:11).

 PRACTICAL PROJECT

Start with a small snowball and roll it around in the yard. See how big you can make it. Chart how many days it takes to melt.

Assign each member of the family a daily chore. How many days does it take before it becomes a habit?

Crystal Growth

Falling Snow

Snowflakes forming in high atmosphere only increase in size while falling at a speed of about five feet per second. When each flake reaches earth it dissolves into moisture. This may become spring runoff to promote growth, or may be part of an avalanche causing destruction.

John Ruskin said this of childhood: "The whole period of adolescence is one essentially of formation, education, and instruction. There is not an hour of it but is trembling with destiny. Not a moment of it once passed the appointed work can ever happen again, or the neglected blow to be stuck on cold iron."

As a snowflake forms while falling, so a child's character forms while toddling. This urgency of childhood is what drives mothers almost to distraction, while forming the next generation! Moses' mother knew she had but 12 years of influence. How urgent her moments.

One boy spent most of his time playing ball and games. When a young adult, he sadly discovered there is no need for mediocre ball players.

Through adolescence and teen years another boy rode around on a motorcycle. He said, "It was my single goal, joy, and ambition." He painfully discovered as a young man, there is little demand for motorcycle drivers.

In the early 1900s a third boy, Willy, received a gift of a microscope on his 15th birthday. It was snowing and he took his gift outside and captured a snowflake. Thus began his life's work. For the following 50 years he photographed snowflakes. As a farm boy with no formal education or training, he photographed over 6,000 perfect snow crystals. He was Wilson J. Bentley, known world over for his contribution to science.

"Lost yesterday, somewhere between sunrise and sunset, two golden hours, each set with 60 diamond minutes. No reward is offered. They are gone forever," said Horace Mann.

Solomon said it this way, "Remember now your Creator in the days of your youth, before the difficult days come, and the years draw near when you say, 'I have no pleasure in them'" (Ecclesiastes 12:1).

 ### PRACTICAL PROJECT

Lay on your back and watch snowflakes float earthward. How long a journey did they take before landing like a feather on your nose? With a pocket magnifying glass examine these cold jewels. Their size and design tell the story of their life. Like snow, a child's trip is just begun. What story will it tell? "Uphold my steps in Your paths, that my footsteps may not slip" (Psalm 17:5).

Falling Snow

Pollution

Our atmosphere normally holds about a ten-day supply of fresh water suspended in the air by way of vapor. It is also filled with living and dead material such as dust, ash, soot, salt, sand, pollen, bacteria, and sand crystals from the oceans. Star dust also falls into our atmosphere. It has been estimated that about 3,000 tons bombard our earth each day. Our world also spins off about the same amount into space, thus maintaining a balance.

The air we breathe is getting dirty. Cars in America discharge approximately 280,000 tons of pollutants into the atmosphere each day.

God takes the very dust itself with which to give the air a bath. Each little snow crystal starts with a nucleus. It may be dust from a farmer's field, volcano, exhaust gas, or a broken part of another snowflake. If they are the right temperature and if there is an excess of water vapor, a crystal will form around the nuclei and thus a snow crystal is born.

If God can so clothe a particle of dust or salt, and make it into a thing of beauty, what can He do with your life and mine? "Now to Him who is able to do exceedingly abundantly above all that we ask or think, according to the power that works in us, to Him be glory in the church by Christ Jesus through out all ages, world without end. Amen" (Ephesians 3:20, 21).

Likewise God has provided a purifier for unconverted hearts: "How can a young man cleanse his way? By taking heed according to Your word ... Your word I have hidden in my heart, that I might not sin against You" (Psalm 119:9, 11).

God would also have us cultivate a love for strict cleanliness in our homes.

Rain and snow are nature's air filters. They help cleanse the air of pollutants that are in the air about us.

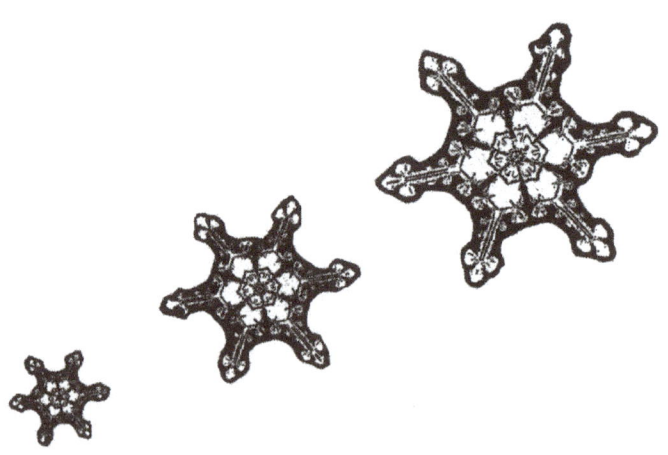

 PRACTICAL PROJECT

Stand outside right after a snowfall and smell the air. What does it smell like? If pure snow falls through dirty air how much dirt will it collect? With an adult, gather a large pan of snow and heat it on the stove until it melts. How much dirt is seen floating on the surface or settled on the bottom? Look at the melted snow water with a magnifying glass or microscope. How would Philippians 4:8 work as a filter for thoughts that come into our minds via television, books, and music or any other media?

Pollution

Mysterious Hexagon

Fifteen centuries before the birth of Christ, God challenged Job, "Have you entered the treasury of snow?" (Job 38:22).

Aristotle took up the challenge four hundred years before the birth of Christ when he observed: "When a cloud freezes there is snow."

In 1611, the year the King James Version of the Bible was first published, a mathematician named Johann Keplar wrote a book on snow. It was a gift to his king entitled *Six-Cornered Snowflake: A New Year's Gift*. As a mathematician he 'twists his brain all out of shape' trying to answer the question, "Why does a snowflake have six sides?" Why does it not have seven, eight, or ten sides?

At the end of the book he leaves the question unanswered by saying, "Let's ask the chemist; maybe he can help."

Snow is still a puzzle to modern minds. Keplar's puzzle of why six sides still remains a modern challenge.

The snow crystal is a three-dimensional geometrical consistent design. How a snow crystal is generated in a universe supposedly dominated by random accidental happenings is a puzzle to evolutionists. The evolutionists believe everything happened by chance, contrary to God's Word. When commenting on why snow has six sides, scientist Lancelot Law Whyte expected science to have a simple explanation when he says, "We should not expect complete knowledge of highly complex systems, but it is reasonable to require of science a simple explanation of simple observations." He goes on to ask: "What in the ultimate laws produces visually perfect patterns?"

The design of snow tells of a Designer who originated the laws by which the patterns and designs are made.

 ## PRACTICAL PROJECT

Go to page 55 and try your hand at restoring a snow crystal. Feel free to photocopy the page so each family member can have their own instructions. How hard is it to restore a beautiful snowflake? The half-restored insert shows how this crystal can be restored. You drew a flat snowflake. Think about how difficult it would be to create that snowflake in three dimensions, each one a unique design. We can thank our Designer for the beautiful patterns that He has given us in the natural world. Enjoy!

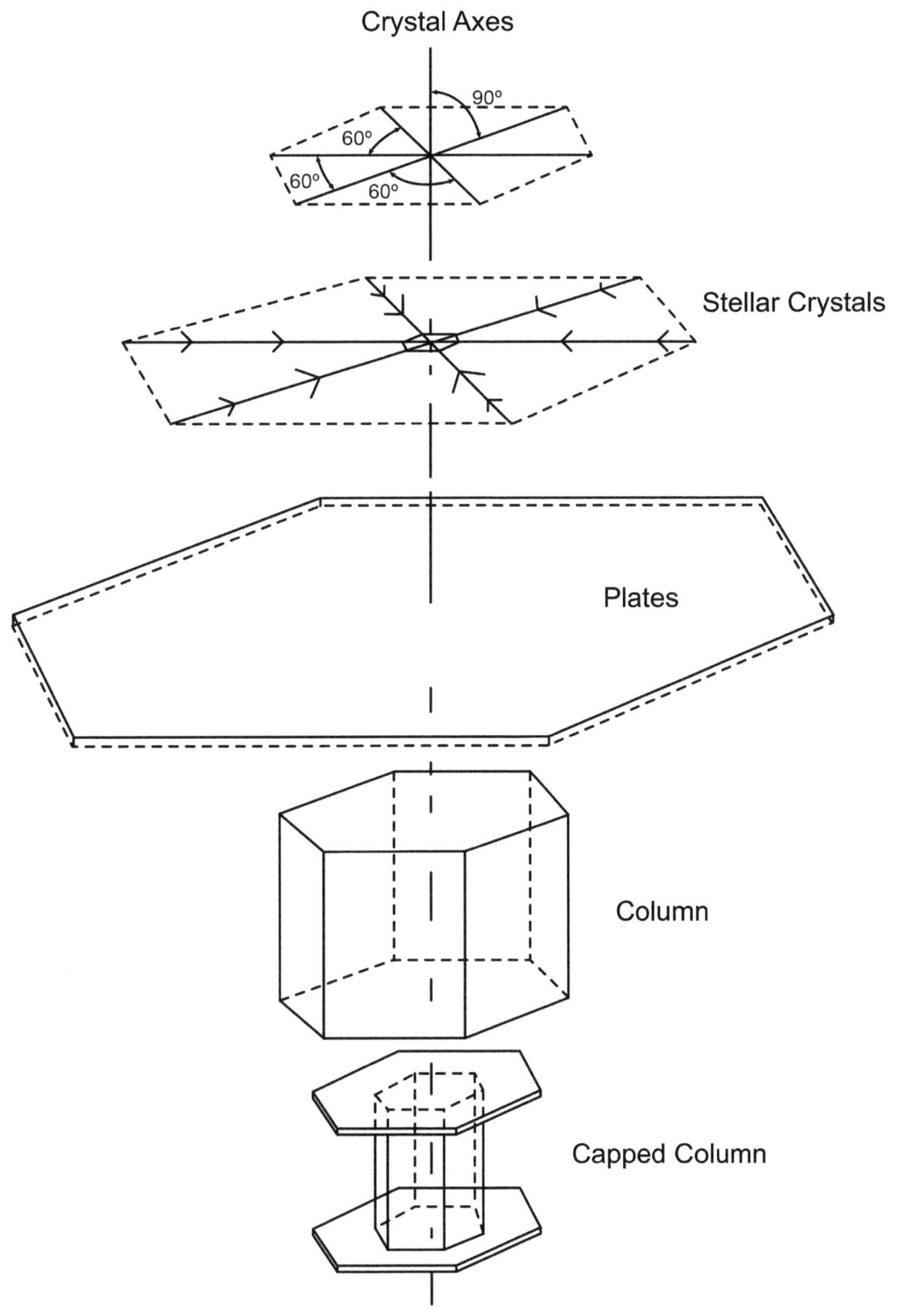

Frozen Individuality

Snowflakes appear almost alive with unlimited variety of design. No two are exactly alike for no two take the same journey from the clouds to earth. God not only loves beauty; He also loves individuality.

Ukichiro Nakaya, a Japanese scientist, devoted his whole life to the study of snow at Hokkaido University. He learned by trial and error how to grow synthetic snow crystals in his cold chamber laboratory. Here he has identified seventy-nine categories of snow crystals and added one column for miscellaneous. He discovered that the slightest change in temperature, up or down, will change the form of a growing crystal. No one yet knows precisely how or why this happens. He says that snowflakes are letters from the sky, enabling us to read the weather above.

In 1951, the International Commission of Snow and Ice proposed a classification recognizing seven basic forms of snow crystals.

In the high clouds of 0° Fahrenheit or -17° Celsius, there are many tiny triangular shapes. They are not heavy enough yet to fall. The air contains water vapor of tiny droplets so small it would take about a million of them to make a single raindrop. These droplets of water condense around a microscopic bit of dust. Thus begins the snow crystal's unique individuality. The slightest change in either temperature or moisture will change the shape of its design.

Beautiful snowflake crystals remind us of a profound truth that we have not made ourselves. "Know that the Lord, He is God; It is He who had made us, and now we ourselves; We are His people and the sheep of His pasture" (Psalm 100:3). You are never to lose your uniqueness or individuality to that of another. God is the owner of your individuality. My ears may be larger than yours and your eyes may be a different color. However, these characteristics are marks of God's ownership. "I will praise You, for I am fearfully and wonderfully made" (Psalm 139:14).

 ## PRACTICAL PROJECT

As a family go outside in the next snowstorm and see how many different kinds of snow crystals can be gathered. Try to identify the weather above by the type of crystal. If the crystal is small in size there is little moisture above. If they are large in size there is warmer moist air above. Use the shapes of crystals in the following chart to help you "read" the weather. In Appendix 1, you can learn how to make your own snowflake. Enjoy!

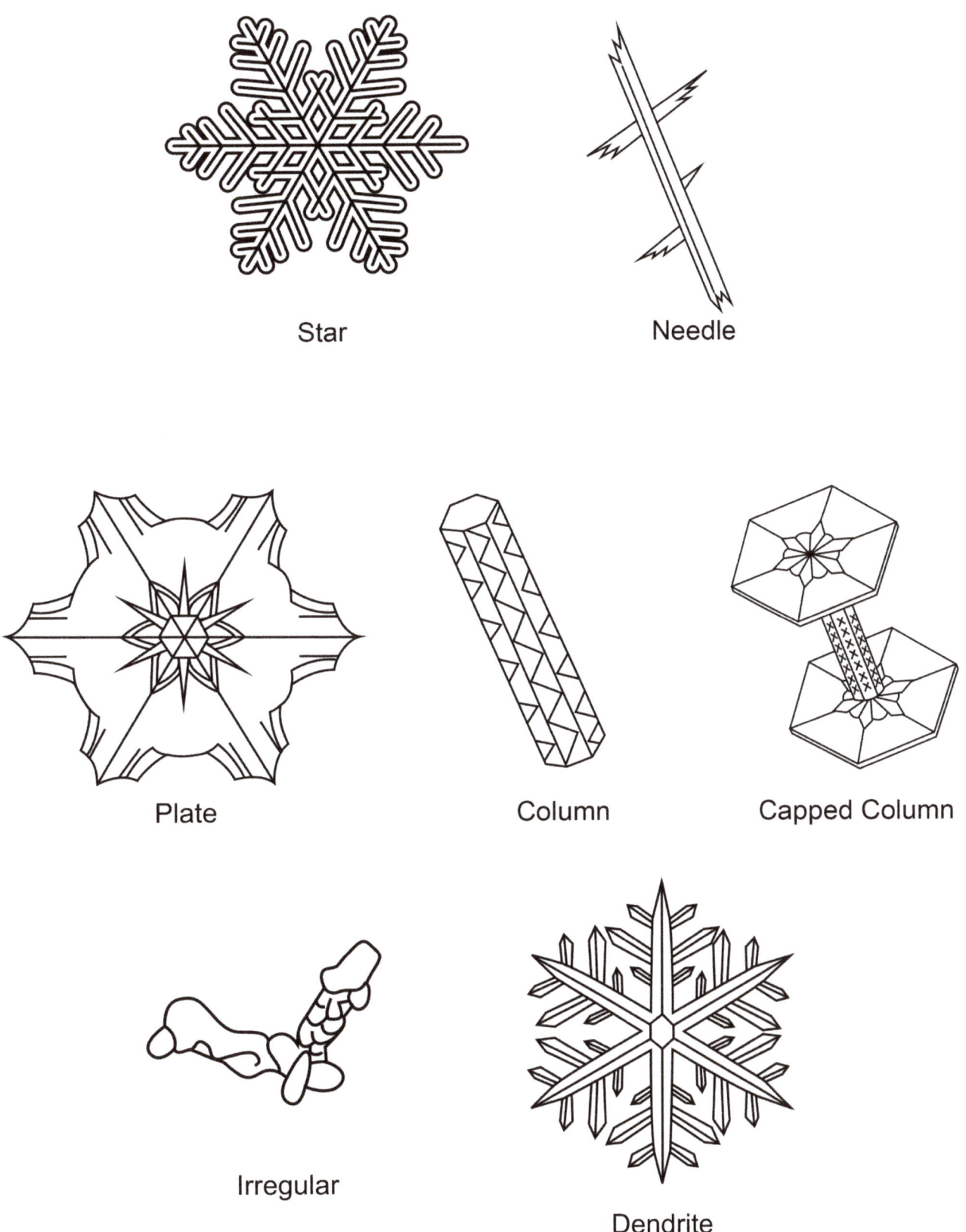

Six-Sided Crystal

A bit of wind-blown dust becomes the center of a snow crystal. Droplets of water vapor crystalize around it forming a perfect hexagon shape.

The snow crystal grows in size as it falls through the air. This finger-like growth happens on the sides of the hexagon as moisture crystalizes there. Each of the six fingers or rays connect together in the middle of the crystal around the bit of dust.

These rays are separated one from the other by exactly 60 degrees. This separation of 60 degrees is caused by what I call "The Divine Law of the Snow Crystal." Obedience to this law is what gives snow its beautiful hexagon pattern.

This law of a snow crystal and the law of God have the same Author. The law of God is a law of love. We are commanded to love one another. The way we love one another is crystalized for us in the last six commandments. See Mark 10:19. These six laws connect together in the great center, Jesus. "I have kept My Father's commandments and abide in His love" (John 15:10).

1. When you receive Christ's love you will desire to honor the parents who procreated you by God's power.
2. You will preserve your right, and my right, to live.
3. You will be morally pure.
4. You will respect another's right to ownership.
5. You will be honest and true to everyone.
6. You will be grateful and contented with what you have because all of us are special objects of His love and everything we have and are comes from God's hand. Within these laws you are free to be you and I am free to be me. James calls it, "the law of liberty" (James 2:12).

Whenever you destroy one of God's commandments you lose some of your freedom and force someone else to lose a bit of theirs. Within these six points of divine design beautiful freedom is guaranteed for all! If God can make such beauty with the 60 degree law of snow crystals, think what He can do with humans who willingly live His law of love.

 PRACTICAL PROJECT

Draw a hexagon—6 equally sided triangles. List the last 6 of the Ten Commandments (see Exodus 20), placing one commandment per side on your hexagon. How do these 6 commands preserve the individuality of each family member? Discuss this together.

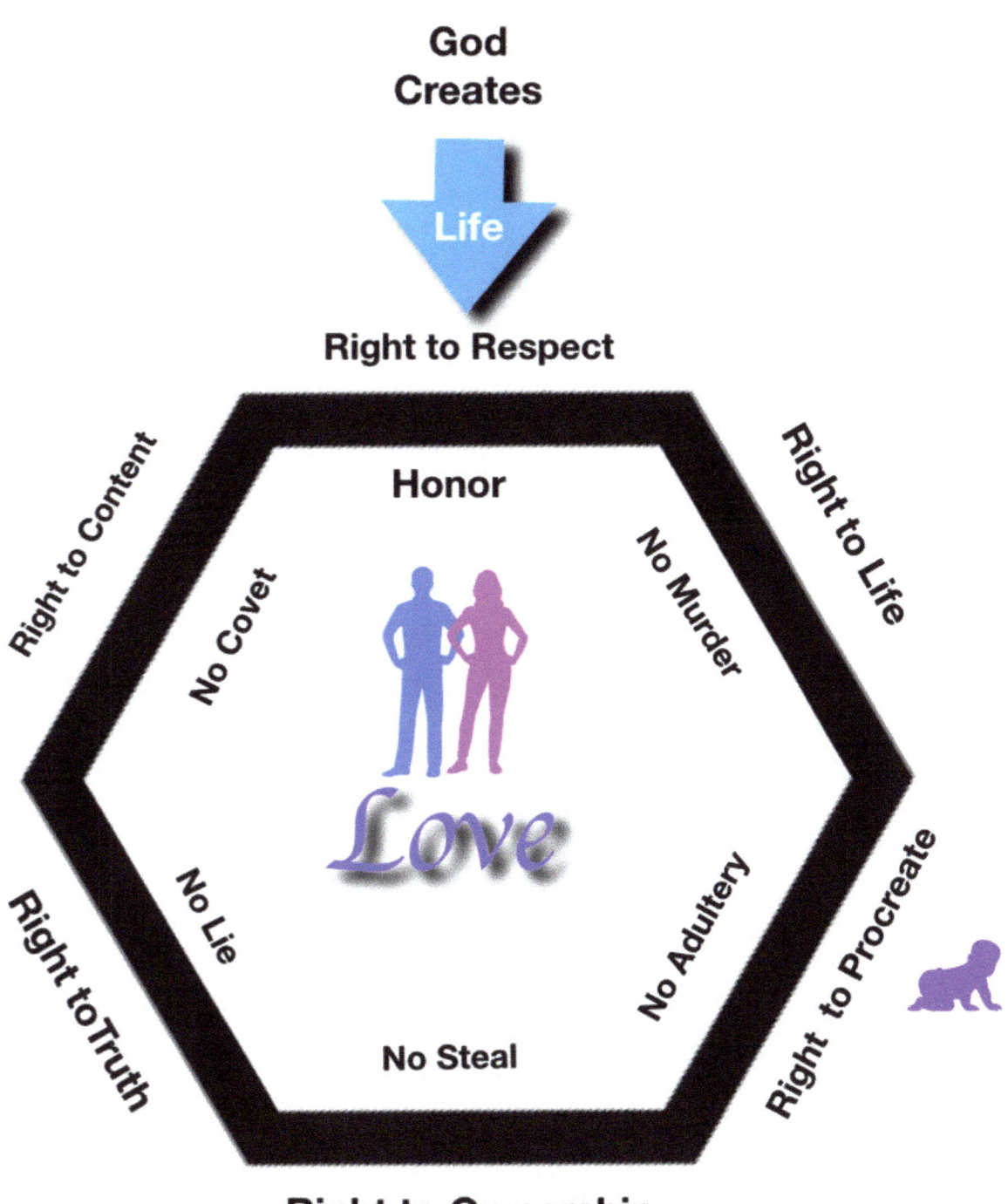

A Little Thing

Snowflakes are cold, temporary little things. They testify of God and teach us that nothing is beneath the notice of our Infinite Creator. This frozen bit of moisture following its crystalline six-sided design demonstrates something of the perfection of our Maker. Meteorologist Vincent J. Schaefer has calculated that it takes more than a million crystals to blanket a two-foot square area with snow ten inches deep. Snowflakes are little things; but when accumulated they can bring all modernized machinery to a standstill. Remember: an avalanche can bury a village and stop a train.

Likewise little things in our lives add up for good or bad. Each member of the family may exercise such little things as gentleness, kindness, carefulness, and patience. Each can do his best to lighten little burdens of father and mother, by putting things away or drying dishes etc. Some may excuse themselves from their duty leaving to others that which they should and could do. These little things are small, but when added together they can create and avalanche of disorder.

The Creator of the snowflake faithfully designed the six sides of a snow crystal by His on-going laws. "He who is faithful in what is least is faithful also in much; and he who is unjust in what is least is unjust also in much" (Luke 16:10). The Creator of the snowflake is none other than Jesus Christ. Paul declares, "And He is before all things, and in Him all things consist" (Colossians 1:17). In fact Jesus not only creates snowflakes, but He also created the heavens and earth with the same care. "For by Him [Jesus] all things were created that are in heaven and that are on earth, visible and invisible, whether thrones or dominions or principalities or powers. All things were created through Him and for Him" (Colossians 1:16).

The entire natural world shows that Jesus gave careful attention to the little things. Perfectly designed snow crystals are proof.

 FAMILY PROJECT

As a family try making a snow sculpture. This is best done when the temperature is just above freezing. Fresh-fallen snow is 90–95% air. Compressed snow can be compared to light concrete. Use your imagination to create creatures or other objects of your choice. Snow packed hard is best for carving. Garden tools can be used to create shapes. Use cake coloring in spray bottles to add color and water in spray bottle to add hardness to ice to hold it in place. Use gelatin molds, mixing bowls, metal-baking pans etc. to add neat shapes. Use natural objects like pinecones, needles, berries, rocks, fallen branches, and fabric in your creation. Try a spiritual theme from the Bible as a witness to the neighborhood. Outdoor colored lighting for light and shadow effects for night viewing can be the crowning touch to your creativity.

A Little Thing

Stored Snow

The U. S. Department of Agriculture has been doing snow surveys every year since 1935. Depth of snow in mountains tells how much water will be available in the valley for next summer's crops. In 1976 a record setting snowfall of 199 inches fell in Buffalo, New York. On the mountains of northern California 189 inches fell in a single snowstorm. Mount Rainier in Washington State once received over a hundred feet of snow in one year. If that amount falls at one time, it could cover a nine-story building!

If given the choice, would you drink water from a glacier-fed stream in the mountain or a sewer polluted river in the valley? God asks this very question. "Will a man leave the snow-water of Lebanon, which comes from the rock of the field? Will the cold flowing waters be forsaken for strange waters?" (Jeremiah 18:14).

God invites us to see His works in the natural world. He desires to turn our mind from the study of the artificial to the natural. God would lead us to His original source for our learning—to that which is God-made: the snow-waters of Lebanon, rather than strange waters of self-centered humanism. Some books and DVDs artificially take what God made and try to give its glory to man. This is often true in the area of natural science. Science fiction is a confused blending of some truth and much error. Evolution is truly science fiction.

Schools often exalt mere human speculation to a place of authority above the pure Word of God. The teaching of evolution is one example of this. How privileged we are to have access to God's "word of truth" (2 Timothy 2:15).

Television, at times, can be compared to an open end of a sewer pipe in our living room. With its fictional stories, TV's polluted streams from Hollywood can only give our family a make-believe approach to real life.

Snow is God's means to store moisture, holding it in reserve until springtime. As temperatures warm in spring, snow melts, producing spring runoff. Abundance of water arrives in our valley on time to produce summer's growth.

Whatever gets our attention is permanently stored in our subconscious mind. These memories will become part of our "spring runoff" in our words, actions, and everyday choices.

"Out of the abundance of the heart the mouth speaks" (Matthew 12:34).

PRACTICAL PROJECT

Keep your own family record of the snowfall where you live.
Materials needed: a bucket or can 10 inches high, a piece of masking tape the same length, waterproof marker, paper for charting, pencil, ruler. Place tape on the inside of the bucket from the bottom to the top, with markings one inch apart and numbered accordingly. Look at the bucket after each snowfall. Write down how much snow fell and then empty the bucket. At the end of the winter add up all the numbers on your chart.

Whiter than Snow

The color of snow is white. But what makes snow white? How white is snow?

Actually snow has no color of its own. It is transparent. The angle of the crystal structure reflects light so it appears white. Snow is totally dependent on light outside itself to reflect the color of white.

When the bright fall colors fade to a drab brown, how we wait for the first snow to make the world pretty again. Snow covers the earth with a robe of reflected light. We may feel like the drab brown of earth at times in our innermost soul. There is a craving—a desire and longing for something better—an unsatisfied desire for wholeness and fulfillment. This hungering and thirsting for God is awakened in our hearts by the Holy Spirit.

God offers to satisfy this inner soul hunger with His cleansing promise: "Though your sins are like scarlet, they shall be as white as snow" (Isaiah 1:18). Changing scarlet to white is a BIG change. Scarlet sins originate with the "me first" principle. It says, "I want what I want, and I don't care who gets hurt." It is immaturity; it is selfishness. See 1 John 3:4.

David understood this selfishness when his guilt drove him to plead with God, "Wash me, and I shall be whiter than snow" (Psalm 51:7). Notice God is here asked to do the washing. "Whiter than snow" is a prayer, not for mere forgiveness, but for cleansing.

When we are willing to be cleansed of selfishness, God is able. "If we confess our sins, He is faithful and just to forgive us our sins and to cleanse us from all unrighteousness" (1 John 1:9). Confession is admitting our selfish nature to Jesus. As our "sin bearer" He takes our selfish nature and replaces it with His pure, divine love. This love creates righteousness and it produces right thinking.

Thus, we are clothed with the light of His life. His life is reflected in our human clay in the form of right behavior. This behavior is His righteousness. "I will greatly rejoice in the Lord, My soul shall be joyful in my God; for He has clothed me with garments of salvation, He has covered me with the robe of righteousness" (Isaiah 61:10).

PRACTICAL PROJECT

Purchase a prism from an educational store. Angle the prism toward the sun in such a way that the multi-colored light will be reflected off a light-colored wall or paper. This is best done in a darkened room with a small hole letting in one single ray of light. Place the prism in this ray and then the colors become visible. Count how many colors you see. If we confess our wrongs and keep our consciences clean and white, we will reflect Jesus' multi-faceted love from within. Its first visible manifestation will be seen in the way we love each other at home.

Snow Changes Things

Snow brings many changes to God's wonderful world of nature. The snowshoe rabbit, the snowy owl, the ptarmigan, the weasel, and the vole are all little creatures that change the coloring of their fur and feathers to match the color of the snow. This adaptation enables them to blend well into the snowy society where they live. How did they acquire this skill?

We can change black hair into white by simply living long enough. We have not learned how to change it back to black again naturally. The animals yearly changing of color is a little miracle we take almost for granted. This skill is given by God to aid the creatures in a changed white world.

Weasels have been seen going in and out of the snow, jumping for the sheer joy of it. When cold comes, birds migrate. Insects cycle to dormancy during snow time. Moose and elk with long legs get around quite well in snow. Buffalo or bison bulldoze their way through snow. Mountain sheep and goats stay high in the mountains.

Children love playing in snow. God is pleased when His creatures are happy. He delights in the simple natural pleasures of both creature and man. Snow and conversion are both gifts of our gracious Heavenly Father designed to bless and make us happy.

How shall we become changed in order to fit into a heavenly society where there is no sin? "But we all, with unveiled face, beholding as in a mirror the glory of the Lord, are being transformed into the same image from glory to glory, just as by the Spirit of the Lord" 2 Corinthians 3:18. One of the signs of conversion is when we stop trusting our own wisdom and start trusting Christ. "Therefore, if anyone is in Christ, he is a new creation; old things have passed away; behold, all things have become new" (2 Corinthians 5:17). Conversion is ceasing to trust in the flesh and learning to trust in what the Spirit will do for us. That is a miracle. The miracle of conversion is greater than the miracle the animals display, when their fur or feathers turn to white every winter.

As a born-again Christian we put on a robe of His righteousness, which becomes visible in the way we love one another.

FAMILY FUN

Play Fox and Geese as a family in the snow. Foxes chase the geese. The geese get a 15-minute head start to find a place to hide. Try to find a way to cover your tracks! Use white clothing, hats, and mittens, or try using an old sheet to help you hide. Have fun!

Snow Changes Things

Snow Armaments

God may use snow as one of His weapons to overrule in the battles of men to the ultimate honor of God. "Have you entered the treasury of snow, or have you seen the treasury of hail, which I have reserved for the time of trouble, for the day of battle and war?" (Job 38:22, 23).

Hitler discovered something of the horrors of God's armaments when he ran into the white cold of a Russian winter in World War II. Hannibal with his elephants incurred great losses in the Alps because of snow. Alexander the Great in 330 BC could not go into India because of snow. Pharaoh learned something about the power of God's armaments in Exodus 9:23, 25, 26. "And Moses stretched out his rod toward heaven; and the Lord sent thunder and hail, and fire darted to the ground. And the Lord rained hail on the land of Egypt.... And the hail struck throughout the whole land of Egypt, all that was in the field, both man and beast; and the hail struck every herb of the field. Only in the land of Goshen, where the children of Israel were, there was no hail." When God chooses, there is a marked difference in those who follow the Lord and those who are at war with Him.

The Amorites also discovered too late what it means to try to fight with the God of creation. In Joshua 10:11 we discover more of them died from the hail stones than from the children of Israel who slew with the sword. Sin has forced God into war. War is so out of character with God that the Bible refers to His war as the "wrath of the Lamb" (Revelation 6:16). Lambs are not ordinarily angry. However, in Revelation 16:21 God warns of a day when He will use gigantic hail stones on His enemies. How awful it would be to be found fighting the God who gave us life and Who has redeemed us.

 FAMILY FUN

Build two snow forts within throwing distance of each other. Make snowballs, loosely packed, and attempt to hit the member at the opposite fort. When hit, you are out. Last person standing is king of the forts.

Snow Armaments

Warm Snow

Cold snow preserves warmth when laid down as a blanket on earth. Freshly fallen snow is about 90% trapped air, making it very fluffy. Trapped air in the snow acts like insulation, shielding the earth below from the frigid air above. In colder climates snow does not melt before the next snow falls so it is laid down layer upon layer. Imagine several blankets piled on top of one another, the bottom layer is the first snowfall. This bottom layer is made up of enlarged and loosely spaced snow crystals with angular corners. Closely examined, many of these crystals are beautiful hollow pyramids, made of miniature crystal logs. This is called depth hoar or pukak.

The air temperature may be a -24° Fahrenheit. Near the top of the snow blanket the reflected light warms the air to a little below zero° Fahrenheit. Under the deep snow near the earth, the temperature may be only freezing or even slightly warmer. Small creatures such as mice, shrew, and vole all bask in this trapped warmth under the snow blanket above. They build a subterranean society with little tunnels going every which way beneath the protective snow.

Russians, in a comparative study, discovered frost would penetrate less than an inch under six inches of snow. Soil not covered by snow froze to a depth of one foot. Below the snow surface soil maintains an even temperature.

Our spiritual life can be kept at an even temperature by the faith of Jesus. When Jesus was a boy, He was able to have peace, even when others rejected Him, or when He was opposed and treated very cruelly. Jesus will give us this peace if we ask Him. "You (Jesus) will keep him in perfect peace, whose mind is stayed on You, because he trusts in You" (Isaiah 26:3). This faith can protect us from fear or anxiety when evil seems to be chilling our personal atmosphere.

 ## FAMILY PROJECT

Find a snowbank that is three feet dep. Carefully cut the snow with a flat shovel or saw, down to the earth. Can you see the different snow layers? Examine the snow crystals at the bottom with a magnifying glass, then those at the top. How do they differ?

Place a thermometer in an ice cube tray and freeze in the freezer. On a day when it is sub zero, take it outside and leave there for an hour. Note that insulating ice will keep the temperature in the ice cube tray the same, even though the temperature outside is much colder.

Warm Snow

Tracks in the Snow

It is fun to play detective when there are tracks in the snow. Animals and birds leave their footprints in the snow. We can tell who has been there and what they were doing by the tracks they leave behind.

Tracks in the snow accurately tell what animal has been there and the path it took. Take a walk in a park or woods as a family after a new snowfall and see how many different tracks of birds or animals you find. Try to identify them.

When we use the telephone it leaves an electronic track telling who we called and how long we talked. In the computer world on the internet we also leave electronic tracks telling which web site we went to and how long we were there.

Parents, are our daily footprints safe for our children to follow? Can our younger children safely follow in the steps of older brother and sister? "Ponder well the path of your feet" (Proverbs 4:26).

Elk, deer, and moose with their long legs get around well in the snow; but when the snow becomes waist deep they walk single file, one following the other. In this way well beaten paths are formed in the snow. These paths provide them a quick escape if pursued by a predator.

In a similar way children tend to follow one another. Group pressure at school inclines us to follow one another in dress, diet, language, and other habits. This may be dangerous. Scripture cautions, "You shall not follow a crowd to do evil" (Exodus 23:2). The majority vote is not always safe. "There is a way which seems right to a man, but its end is the way of death" (Proverbs 14:12). Every person thinks his way is right. See Proverbs 21:2. There are many voices saying follow me. How can we know the right way? "In all your ways acknowledge Him, and He shall direct your paths" (Proverbs 3:6).

How I live each day leaves a trail behind. My use of time is like footprints revealing habit patterns showing if I am following Him who said, "I am the way, the truth, and the life" (John 14:6).

FAMILY PROJECT

Make a large circle in the snow. Now cut the circle in 8 or so pieces like cutting a pie. When completed, the leader goes to the center of the circle. He becomes IT. He now will try to catch any of the other family players who have scattered all around the outside of the circle. The key rule of the game is you must stay within the lines. If anyone runs outside the lines while being chased they are now IT. All will have to run when one is chased. What affects one affects all. This game teaches cooperation and the importance of staying with the lines (the laws) even when pursued.

Tracks in the Snow

Frozen Reservoirs

Three-fourths of the earth's fresh water is stored in the vast glaciers of this world, such as the wastelands of the Antarctic seen on the opposite page. Both the North Pole and South Pole are snow covered deserts. They receive only two inches of snow per year. This snow falls as separate crystals, so fine that they look like snow dust, and none of it ever melts. These frozen reservoirs contain an estimated 75 years' worth of snow and rain for the whole world at the present rate of consumption.

When old snow is buried year after year by newer snow, the weight crushes the lower layers into compressed ice. Once it reaches a depth of 60 feet thick it will begin to flow slowly downhill. If these slow-moving, bluish rivers of solid ice reach the sea they break off into icebergs.

Snow can compact into an ice pack reaching a depth of 1,000 feet or more. Most of this permanent snow lies at the North and South Pole. Snow covers approximately half of the land's surfaces on our planet at least temporarily and about 10% of the ocean surface. Some 48 million square miles of the earth's surface lie under a constant blanket of snow.

It has been calculated the South Pole, or the Antarctic, is half again as large as the United States. Coal and petrified tree trunks indicate that the Antarctic once had a much warmer climate. Three flowers actually grow there: gentians, buttercups, and calceolarias. One animal, the Emperor Penguin, lives there also. Geologists have pieced together evidence of distinct periods when snow and ice blanketed a far greater part of the earth than it does now. It is possible that this was caused by the tilting of the earth at the time of the flood. Fossil evidence shows tropical vegetation and animal life once lived at the North and South Pole before the flood.

I have hung 15 feet down into a glacier crack suspended by a rope. Beautiful blue glacial ice merged into black obscurity below and on either side. My only hope of rescue came from above when my teammates pulled me back to the glacier surface.

In a similar way our world needs a Savior. The antediluvian (before the flood) world became so wicked that God in mercy had to destroy it with a flood. Jesus said, "But as the days of Noah were, so also will the coming of the Son of Man be" (Matthew 24:37).

 FAMILY PROJECT:

Make your own glacier. Take a glass quart jar outside and let the snow collect into the jar. Later, put the jar into the freezer to keep it frozen. Next time it snows, take it outside and add the next layer of snow. Do this all winter and you will have your own glacier. You will be able to see all the layers of snow that fell throughout the winter. This project should start with the first winter snowfall since snow will be collected throughout the season.

Perito Moreno Glacier, located in Los Glaciares National Park, Argentina

Crystallized Vapor

Snow is not frozen water but crystallized water vapor. Cold air holds little water vapor because it crystallizes. Water vapor goes directly into a crystalline form (without becoming a liquid) to form snow crystals high in the clouds. When man makes snow using machines, he uses frozen water.

Snow guns are used on ski slopes to produce snow when the air is below freezing. A stream of cooled water is split into many tiny droplets by compressed air. These droplets freeze into ice as they fall through the chilled air. Some snow machines have special cooling units to help make snow when air is not cold enough outside.

Water is made up of two parts hydrogen and one part oxygen, referred to as H2O. Spiritually this formula works this way: the two Hs stand for heavenly and human and the O stands for others. When the heavenly and human unite in service to others, the grace of the Holy Spirit will clothe the dust of the human clay with a beauty of divine design. When we confess that "without Him we can do nothing" (John 15:5), we shall reflect the "light that lights every light" (John 1:9). Thus we become like Jesus said, "You are the light of the world" (Matthew 5:14).

If God can so clothe a speck of dust with His divine design of crystallized vapor, what can the same Creator do with a willing, intelligent human clothed with His Holy Spirit? Some youth worry they may lose their individuality when they surrender soul, mind, and body to Christ. Look at the infinite designs of snowflake. The same Creator made each person an individual, unique and special. Instead of losing individuality, it is developed "abundantly beyond all that we can ask or think" (Ephesians 3:20). There is no limit to what one can become when self is set aside and room is made for the working of the Holy Spirit.

FAMILY PROJECT

Snowball Lantern: This cool lantern gives good light. It is attractive when placed by your sidewalk if you are having company over in the evening. Materials needed: 8–10 snowballs and a candle or flashlight. Snowballs are placed in the form of a circle at the bottom layer. Then the next layer is superimposed over the first, edging slightly closer to the center. You will end up with about five layers. Be sure to add your candle or flashlight before you add the last layers.

Crystallized Vapor

Divine Design

Fresh fallen snow sparkles with hues of a rainbow. Light reflects off the crystal snowflakes like radiant jewels from a hidden treasure. Our Creator invites us to slow down with the rest of the natural world and enjoy this cold beauty. Some become so wrapped up in skiing, sledding parties, and snowmobiling they almost worship fun in snow more than its Creator.

People speak of mother nature as though nature created herself. Nature about us is controlled by what we call natural law. An example of natural law is the law of gravity. God did not create our world, set it spinning, and then leave it to operate on its own. It is by the direct agency of God that nature continues to operate. "And He is before all things and in Him all things consist" (Colossians 1:17). He commands snow to fall.

Our world is sustained by His ongoing commands. His mighty power works through all nature maintaining things by His divine activating energy.

The marvelous handiwork of nature is not God. Nature is an expression of God's skill. By it we understand something of His love, power, and glory. (See Romans 1:20.) But nature is not God. The artist who drew the pictures in this book created beautiful work; but the thing drawn is not the artist. The workman is worthy of honor. Nature is an expression of God's thoughts. Not nature, but the God of nature, is to be honored and exalted.

Nature is beautiful because it does not resist God's laws, but rather obeys them. Who is this Creator who made our world beautiful? Even in the wintertime? "God, who at various times and in different ways spoke in time past to the fathers by the prophets, has in these last days spoken to us by His Son, whom he has appointed heir of all things, through whom also He made the worlds" (Hebrews 1:1, 2).

This Designer-Artist who made this world and keeps it spinning is none other than Jesus. With delight and gratitude we can go walking through His natural world. Obedience to His laws and on-going commands reveal the skill and handicraft of the Creator who laid down His life for His creatures. Snow is a gift of God's love. Let us not take this gift of mercy for granted and worship the gift; but worship the Giver.

 FAMILY PROJECT:

Make Sparkling Snow Paint: Mix ½ cup flour, ½ cup salt, ½ cup water. After mixing these ingredients, put them in a squeeze bottle to use as paint on black construction paper. Paint a snow scene. Let the paint dry thoroughly and it will sparkle. You may paint again on top after the paint has dried for a more three-dimensional effect.

Divine Design

God Sends Snow

"God thunders marvelously with His voice; He does great things which we cannot comprehend. For he says to the snow, 'Fall on the earth'; Likewise to the gentle rain and the heavy rain of His strength. He seals the hand of every man, that all men may know His work. The animals enter dens, and remain in their lairs. From the chamber of the south comes the whirlwind, and cold from the scattering winds of the north. By the breath of God ice is given, and the broad waters are frozen. Also with moisture He saturates the thick clouds; He scatters His bright clouds. And they swirl about, being turned by His guidance, that they may do whatever He commands them on the face of the whole earth. He causes it to come, whether for correction, or for His land, or for mercy" (Job 37:5–13).

God sends the snow for one of three reasons: **1.** For correction: Storms may force you to change your plans so that God's plans for you may succeed. He sees what we do not see. **2.** For His land: The pastures and farmlands welcome the snow. The snow melts slowly into the ground providing moisture needed for growth of food for man and animal. **3.** For mercy: Because of His mercy, the thick insulating blanket of snow falls before the temperature falls. Snow protects seeds and soil from hard, deep freezes. It may also be in mercy that a storm hits, causing all evening programs to cancel. Thus you find an unexpected evening to re-evaluate the worth of your activities.

The trials and the storms of life often prove your very best blessing.

Your life might even be spared by what appears to be a disappointment. Jacob said, "All these things are against me" (Genesis 42:33). But God had a bigger picture in mind. "All things work together for good to those who love God" (Romans 8:28). It doesn't say "some things" or "most things" or "joyous things" but "ALL things."

 PRACTICAL PROJECT

List the times your family has faced a storm of some kind. Evaluate it in the light of the three reasons why God sends snow. Can you find a hidden blessing in the storm?

United Power

A snow crystal weighs so little that when one falls on your nose, you would never feel it except for wet coldness. Incredibly though, when this little crystal is joined by others it can become very heavy.

If you compact snow hard enough it will turn into solid ice. Many children know how to pack a snowball into an ice ball.

Atmospheric pressure helps compact fresh fallen snow, causing it to shrink from 5 to 3 inches in 5 days, even though the temperature remains freezing and the water content remains the same. The density and weight increases as the air content decreases. Thus one flake when united and pressed together with others will become extremely hard and heavy.

In a similar way 2,000 years ago 12 men and a few believers took the gospel to the then known world. This was done without radio, television, airplanes or cars. "Now when the Day of Pentecost had fully come, they were all with one accord in one place" (Acts 2:1). United together with Christ they changed history. Together they accepted Christ's commission: "Go therefore and make disciples of all the nations, baptizing them in the name of the Father and of the Son and of the Holy Spirit, teaching them to observe all things that I have commanded you; and lo, I am with you always, even to the end of the age" (Matthew 28:19, 20).

Jesus prayed for unity among His followers, "that they all may be one." He desired our unity to be the same as His unity was with His Father. "As you, Father, are in Me, and I in You." This kind of unity will convince our world Jesus really came. "…that the world may believe that You sent Me" (John 17:21).

Just as snow crystals unite with others to form something powerful, so we each add our weight to bring success to God's family today. Each individual, bringing their unique gifts or talents, brings benefit to all. This plan of God will bring success to the whole and will unify and strengthen each other.

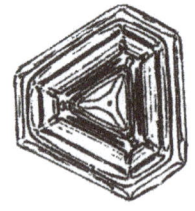

 PRACTICAL PROJECT

Weigh 1 cup of snow after it falls. Next day, measure a cup of the one-day old snow and see how its weight has changed. Do the same on the third day. Notice how the weight changes. We too are changing from day to day. How are you changing from day to day making your weight felt to bring success to your family?

Temporary Snow

A handful of snow will melt quickly when placed on a hot stove. In the west snow melts rapidly when a Chinook wind blows. (Chinook is Native American word which means snow eater). A Chinook can change the air temperature from -40° Fahrenheit to 40° Fahrenheit in a few hours.

Job says the wicked will vanish like melted snow. He compares his wicked friends to ice and snow and says: "When it is warm, they cease to flow: when it is hot, they vanish from their place" (Job 6:17).

You may covet the wealth and fame of the wicked, because for the moment they appear so successful, but you do not see their end. But the wicked, famous, wealthy, and powerful will quickly melt away like snow.

The world today is as temporary as snow. Ours is the NOW generation. The world says, "Buy NOW, pay later," "Enjoy the pleasures of sin for a season." The sin season is short as is the snow season—in the light of eternity. David said: "For evildoers shall be cut off; but those who wait on the Lord, they shall inherit the earth. For yet a little while and the wicked shall be no more; Indeed, you will look diligently for his place, but it shall be no more" (Psalm 37:9, 10). Jesus answered, "My kingdom is not of this world" (John 18:36). His disciples kept trying to make His kingdom of this world. Some of His followers today are still trying to make His kingdom of this world.

But Scripture promises a new heaven and a new earth. "Nevertheless we, according to His promise, look for new heavens and a new earth in which righteousness dwells" (2 Peter 3:13). Our world perished once in a flood of water, Peter tells us in verses 5–8. Our world today is to be destroyed once more, but this time in a flood of fire. (See verse 10.) Our wicked world with its temporary value system will someday vanish like snow in summer's heat.

 ### PRACTICAL PROJECT

With adult supervision, take an old cooking pan and fill it with snow. Heat it on the stove until it melts. How long did it take? Leave pan on heat until all the water is turned into steam and vanishes away. Reread Psalm 37:9, 10. So it will be with the wicked!

Temporary Snow

Pure as Snow

A snow crystal is as clear as glass. Purity is genuine all the way through with nothing hidden.

Our natural world was pure in the beginning of creation. After centuries of decay and degeneration we find even the atmosphere is polluted. Snow was one of the purest forms of natural water. This was before acid rain and air pollution. Paul tells us in Romans 8:21, "Creation itself also will be delivered from the bondage of corruption."

It was through the pollution of sin man lost spiritual purity. This spiritual poverty resulted in pollution of mind and body; because of man's sin, pollution has spread to God's wonderful world of nature. Today it mars even the purity of snow.

Impure magazines may be hidden and read in secret. Lies and darkness may hide secrets, and fool trusting parents. Secrecy, however, does not fool the all-seeing God. A person cannot engage in secret sin and at the same time be at ease.

Trying to clean a polluted river is useless as long as a city continues to dump in raw sewage. In order to have purity we must clean up not only pollution but the cause of pollution.

David prayed for this kind of moral cleansing in Psalm 51:2. Moral impurity is preoccupied with its own selfish desires and cravings. In Matthew 1:19 Jesus warned that our heart is the cause of moral pollution.

Guilty David prayed: "Behold, You desire truth in the inward parts, and in the hidden part You will make me to know wisdom. Purge me with hyssop, and I shall be clean; Wash me, and I shall be whiter than snow… create in me a clean heart, O God, and renew a steadfast spirit within me" (Psalm 51:6, 7, 10). God will wash us from the inside out, whiter than snow. He will remove moral pollution and its cause and replace it with His purity.

🞷 PRACTICAL PROJECT

How pure is snow? With adult supervision, fill a large clean pan with snow, and place on the stove on low heat. When the snow has melted pour the water through a white clean cloth. Note what you see on the cloth! Remember snow is God's air scrubber and it collects pollutants from the air. When Jesus cleanses us, we shall be "Whiter than snow!"

Pure as Snow

White Snow

Holy Scripture has referred to snow 25 times; ten of these times it refers to snow as a white color, for example, whiter than snow. As already noted, snow has no color of itself, but is really transparent. The angle of the crystals makes up the white color.

Many a skier and snowmobiler have discovered painfully how white snow can be when they have forgotten their goggles.

Snow well describes the glorified Jesus. "His head and His hair were white like wool, as white as snow" (Revelation 1:14). "His clothes became shining exceedingly white, like snow, such as no launderer on earth can whiten them" (Mark 9:3).

This brilliancy caused soldiers to fall at Jesus' feet on resurrection morning. Disciples on the mount of transfiguration fell to hide themselves from this blinding light. Stephen's face lighted up as an angel as he preached before the Sanhedrin. See Acts 6:15. Moses' face, after communing with God for 40 days at the time of receiving God's holy law, shone so brightly he had to put on a veil. The very skin of his face shone. See Exodus 34:29.

When Divinity flashed through Jesus' humanity, His own countenance often was lightened up with the light that was divine. We may so commune with Jesus, be so filled with His Spirit, that it may be said of us, "Love has been perfected among us in this: That it may have boldness in the day of judgment; because as he is, so are we in this world" (1 John 4:17).

In attempting to look into the treasures of the snow, we have just touched the tip of the iceberg of the wisdom of God. Our senses are so dull, we see and hear so little as though we had blinders on. We can say with Paul, "For now we see in a mirror, dimly" (1 Corinthians 13:12). Even though hampered by goggles of a sin-weakened body, we can see His treasure in the snow that God is still love.

PRACTICAL PROJECT

God is not finished with us yet! Set aside an afternoon on the day God said was His and enjoy this family fun project of making beautiful paper snowflakes. Listening to inspirational music increases the fun. See page 54.

White Snow

Appendix 1—How to Make Paper Snowflakes

HOW TO CREATE A 6 SIDED SNOW FLAKE

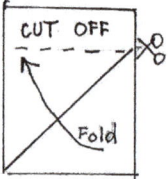

1. START — Make paper square. Fold 8½×11 typing paper diagonally. Cut off top left over.

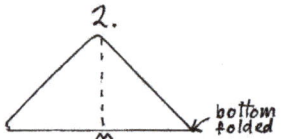

2. Fold the diagonal triangle in half. Then unfold it.

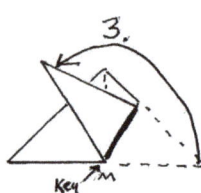

3. Fold right bottom end over the other side of triangle. This is a key fold angle!

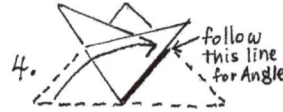

4. Fold left side of triangle over the top of other right fold.

5. Odd shaped object-turn over to backside.

Backside view

6. Now-draw lines you will cut out

7. CUT OUT shaded area

8. CAREFULLY UNFOLD

God creates trillions of these in every snow storm. Psalm 148: 4,5,8

You have created your own 6 sided SnowFlake! Now color it. ENJOY

Appendix 2—How to Restore a Snowflake

An afternoon's project on God's Holy Day. This project is for ages 12 and up and may take more than one Sabbath afternoon to complete. It's very addictive and once started, it's hard to stop! This image is a divine creation created by obedience to the law of six sides. Try your hand as co-creator with God in re-drawing the missing lines in this Bentley photo of a snow crystal. Photocopy this page so each will have their own copy if needed.

Materials needed: Ruler; Fine point 0.1 black pen; Fine pointed paint brush; Black ink; Opaque white-out. **Technique:** Study the parts of the crystal that are clear and restore them where the lines have faded. You add with white what you wish to keep; subtract with black what you wish to remove. Be creative! When finished, frame it and hang it on the wall: a testimony of your human effort united with His divine law. Enjoy!

(This insert shows what a restored snow crystal can look like.)

55

Bibliography

Bentley, W.A., and W.J. Humphreys, *Snow Crystals*. Mineola, NY: Dover Publications, 1962.

La Chapelle, Edward R. *Field Guide to Snow Crystals*. Seattle, WA: University of Washington Press, 1969.

Libbrecht, Kenneth. *The Snowflake, Winter's Secret Beauty*. Vancouver, BC: Whitecap Books Ltd., 2003.

—. Snowcrystals.com. https://1ref.us/1fz (accessed November 11, 2020).

Evans, Eva Knox Evans. *The Snow Book*. Boston, MA: Little, Brown and Company, 1965.

Kirk, Ruth. *Snow*. New York: William Morrow & Company, 1978.

McFall, Christie. *Wonders of Snow and Ice*. New York: Dodd, Mead and Company, 1964.

Lafferty, Peter, and Julian Row. *The Dictionary of Science*. New York: Simon & Schuster, 1994.

March, Daniel. *Our Father's House: Or, the Unwritten Word*. St. Louis, MO: Ziegler & McCurdy, 1869.

Kepler, Johann. *The Six-Cornered Snowflake—A New Year's Gift*. Frankfurt-am-Main: Godfrey Tampach, 1611.

Special Thanks

Special thanks to Kenneth Libbrecht for the permission to use some of his beautiful snow crystal images. His book *The Snowflake, Winter's Secret Beauty* would be a wonderful addition to your library. We highly recommend it!

Subscribe to the Leading Bible-based Nature Journal!

Readers call it, "The Christian answer to National Geographic!"

- Stunning Photography
- Animal & Bird Features
- Creation Science
- Outdoor Travel Adventures
- Gardening Tips
- Youth Photo & Coloring Contests
- Character-building Lessons found in Nature
- Instructional Study Guide
- Even Genesis Cuisine Recipes for healthful living!

UNPLUG and Get Away to Nature & Creation!

4 Quarterly Issues Only $19.95/year–INCLUDES a FREE Digital Subscription
ORDER NOW!
Logon to: www.CreationIllustrated.com or Call: 1(800) 360-2732
or Mail a Check to: Creation Illustrated, PO Box 141103, Spokane Valley, WA 99214

The Gospel According to Creation Seminars

Terry McComb, Speaker and Writer with *Creation Illustrated* magazine, has conducted countless character-building, Bible-based seminars that reveal eternal truths through the handiwork of God. The Spiritual messages have a lasting impact on all ages and include black-light chalk drawings with his wife's soft piano artistry in the background.

Pastor McComb has authored more than 50 articles with *Creation Illustrated* magazine and co-authored with his wife Jean, five children's books for parents to study with their children—*Gospel According to a Dandelion; Gospel According to a Blade of Grass; Gospel According to a Snowflake; Gospel According to a Thornless Blackberry;* and *Gospel According to a Tree.*

Available Seminars (available for purchase as a digital download or DVD copy):

"The Creation Story" is a scientific walk through Genesis one. How does each day of the Creation Week reveal its Author and how is this truth relevant to our spiritual walk? A nine-hour seminar from Sunday through Saturday night.

"In His Image" focuses on the wonder of the human body! This nine-hour seminar is a fast-moving study that examines the 12 systems of the body and their amazing designer. Deeply scientific, yet spiritual.

"The Wonder of a Tree" is a nine-hour seminar illustrating how the lifestyle, function, and ways of a tree reveal the ways of its Creator, Jesus Christ.

"Creations Creator" is a five-hour week-end seminar that addresses evolution vs. creation and the truth about Dinosaurs. Topics include: The Cross as Seen in Nature, Worship Him Who Made, Heart Reading Nature, and the Gospel According to a Dandelion power point presentation with music background.

"How to Heart Read Nature" will help viewers learn how to see past the trees and see the Creator. This is a hands-on practical nine-hour seminar that uses the out-of-doors classroom and needs to be in a nature setting. Short on theory and long on active learning.

"The Heavens are Telling" deals with The Gospel According to Astronomy" with plenty of NASA space telescope photos. This nine-hour seminar shows God's ways in outer space to help fill your heart's inner space with His love.

These Seminars can be done by Zoom
To Book a Seminar or order books and DVD's
Call: (250) 547-6696
E-mail: terry@gospelcreation.com
Web site: www.gospelcreation.com
Write: The Gospel According to Creation Seminar
39 Pine Road, Cherryville, British Columbia, Canada V0E 2G3

TEACH Services, Inc.
PUBLISHING

We invite you to view the complete
selection of titles we publish at:
www.TEACHServices.com

We encourage you to write us
with your thoughts about this,
or any other book we publish at:
info@TEACHServices.com

TEACH Services' titles may be purchased in
bulk quantities for educational, fund-raising,
business, or promotional use.
bulksales@TEACHServices.com

Finally, if you are interested in seeing
your own book in print, please contact us at:
publishing@TEACHServices.com

We are happy to review your manuscript at no charge.

www.ingramcontent.com/pod-product-compliance
Lightning Source LLC
Chambersburg PA
CBHW061604170426
43196CB00039B/2969